DOVER GAME AND PUZZLE ACTIVITY BOOKS

Solve the Mystery
41 Puzzling Cases

WRITTEN BY A. C. GORDON
ADAPTED BY LEWIS AND SANDRA GARDNER

DOVER PUBLICATIONS, INC.
Garden City, New York

Copyright

Bibliographical Note

This Dover edition, first published in 1997, is an unabridged republication of the work first published by Scholastic Book Services, New York, 1976 (as *More Solv-A-Crime*). It is reprinted by special arrangement with Singer Media Corporation, 1030 Calle Cordillera, #106, San Clemente, California 92673.

Library of Congress Cataloging-in-Publication Data

Gordon, A. C.
    [More solv-a-crime]
    Solve the mystery : 41 puzzling cases / written by A.C. Gordon ; adapted by Lewis and Sandra Gardner.
        p.   cm. — (Dover game and puzzle activity books)
    "Singer Media Corporation."
    Originally published under the title: More solv-a-crime. New York : Scholastic Book Services, 1976.
    ISBN-13: 978-0-486-29662-3 (pbk.)
    ISBN-10: 0-486-29662-8 (pbk.)
    1. Puzzles.   2. Detective and mystery stories.   I. Gardner, Lewis.   II. Gardner, Sandra.   III. Singer Media Corporation.   IV. Title.   V. Series.
GV1507.D4C668   1997
793.73—DC21   96-54008
                                                                              CIP

Manufactured in the United States by LSC Communications
29662810   2020
www.doverpublications.com

Contents

The Case of the Attic Arsonist

"What a terrible, unfortunate mess!" exclaims Mrs. Cynthia Coburn, a very wealthy widow. "My family heirlooms in the attic were burned to a crisp. However, I *am* thankful the firemen arrived in time to save the rest of my house.

"If you ask me, I think the fire was set deliberately by my maid, Susan Burns. She claims, of course, that it all happened accidentally. But I have been having a lot of trouble with her recently. She has resented every order that I give her.

"This afternoon I asked her to please go up to the attic to look for some velvet material I had been saving. She mumbled, as usual, but she finally went up the stairs.

"About 15 minutes later she came screaming down the stairs. She told me the whole place was on fire. I phoned the fire department."

A few minutes later you talk with the sullen-looking maid. "It was an accident," she says. "It wouldn't have happened if she let loose some of her money for an electric light in that crummy attic.

"I went up there with a flashlight. When I got there, it wouldn't work—a dead battery. So I used my cigarette lighter to find the right trunk.

"The whole place was loaded with great big cobwebs. They caught fire, flared up, and lit some papers. In a few seconds there was a blazing fire."

"Lucky you were able to get out safely," you say.

The girl nods silently, with a little smile.

"But not lucky enough," you say, "to escape a charge of arson!"

Why do you suspect the maid of arson?

You know that cobwebs do not flame.

1

The Case of the Bashful Bullet

You and Sheriff Regan carefully examine the bullet hole in the lower pane of the living-room window. After gauging the angle of fire, the sheriff nods his head.

You find the shades lowered over the closed windows of the room. You also find Harry Yeager's body slumped in a chair, facing away from the bullet-punctured window.

A .45-caliber bullet went through his head and the window behind him. You estimate that death occurred between 9:00 and 10:00 P.M. It is now 11:35.

You examine the .45-caliber revolver lying on the floor next to the victim. You raise the window shade and see a second bullet hole near the top of the upper windowpane.

"Well, doesn't that beat everything!" the sheriff says. "And only one shot was fired from *this* gun!"

"And here's the bullet," announces Officer Jim Sanders. "I found it in the trunk of the tree just outside the window. It's a .45."

"But two shots must have been fired," says the bewildered sheriff, "even though the gun tells us otherwise. You'd better go back outside and look for that second bullet, Jim. There are those two holes in the window to account for."

"And that is easy to do," you say. "Only one shot was fired."

How do you know that only one shot was fired?

The single shot went through the window while the lower pane was raised or the upper pane was lowered. After the killer fired his shot, he must have closed the window.

The Case of the Body on the Bank

You are stretched out in a hammock in front of your vacation shack. It has been a day with 90% humidity and not a sign of a breeze. Sheriff Jim Travers' arrival signals the end of your relaxation.

"We have a murder on our hands," Travers says. "A couple of hours ago, Bill Sawyer's body was found on the riverbank. He was our local attorney. Shot in the right temple. Judging from the ground near his body, there was a struggle."

"Who discovered the body?" you ask.

"A young fellow named Dick Arlington. The way he tells it, he was on the river in his sailboat, moving slowly upstream, scanning the shores through his binoculars when he suddenly saw the body on the riverbank.

"He started the auxiliary motor on his boat and made straight for the bank. He saw that Sawyer was dead. Then, using the motor again, he piloted his boat to town and reported the murder to me."

"Have you any line on a possible suspect?" you ask.

Travers shakes his head. "I'm afraid not. Bill Sawyer had no enemies around town. I don't know where to begin."

"I think you can start by questioning Dick Arlington again," you say. "I'm sure he knows a lot more about this than he's told you."

What has made you suspicious of Arlington's story?

A sailboat cannot move upstream without "a sign of a breeze." According to Dick Arlington's story, this is what he was doing at the time he saw the victim's body on the bank.

3

The Case of the Bomb in the Bon-Bons

A maid opens the front door of the old mansion. You go upstairs to one of the bedrooms.

Doctor Fleming motions you into the room, nodding his head toward the sheet-covered figure on the bed.

"I phoned you," he says, "because I don't care for the manner in which Mrs. Farrington died."

The doctor picks up a decorated tin candy box from the bedside table. He lifts the hinged lid. You smell the odor of recently discharged powder.

"Some heartless person sent this to the poor old lady," mutters Dr. Fleming. "It was even gift-wrapped. She had an extremely bad heart condition. Everyone knew that. The sudden explosion, when she opened the box, would have frightened anyone out of his wits. For *her* it meant death!"

The doctor shakes his head sadly as he closes the box and puts it back on the table.

A young man hurries into the room. "I just heard about it—poor Aunt Jane! The maid phoned me at work, and I got here as fast as I could."

You ask, "Did the maid tell you the circumstances of your aunt's death?"

"No. Only that some low-down character frightened her to death with some kind of trick."

You tap a finger on the pretty little candy box and say, "This is it—the trick that ended your aunt's life."

The young man looks with horror at the box. "It must have been a dreadful shock to her," he says. "That sudden and unexpected explosion—and with her heart. . . ."

"I imagine you will come into a sizable share of your aunt's fortune," you remark.

"Yes, I think I will." He suddenly stops and fixes you with a startled gaze. "Just what are you trying to say?"

"That right now you are the No. 1 suspect—as the person who hastened your aunt's death!"

Why do you hold this suspicion?

Although the nephew said he had not been informed of the nature of the "trick," he mentioned that it involved a sudden explosion.

The Case of the Brutal Burglar

You are admitted to the posh apartment by a well-known stockbroker, C. Randall Hamilton. It's been a bad week for him. A few days ago, two of his largest corporations went under. And now he's been the victim of a big jewel robbery.

You walk around the living room, looking over the furnishings. You particularly admire the huge, intricately carved cabinet that covers one side of the room. On the shelves are collectors' items, sports trophies, and other knick-knacks. Over it is a mirror, the full length of the cabinet and ceiling-high.

"I suppose you want the whole story now," Hamilton says. You nod, and he begins, "Well, it was my valuable collection of emeralds. An entire tray of them—stones I've been collecting for 15 years. Of course, they're insured. But money can't make up for the loss of the beautiful jewels."

"The story, please," you say.

"I was alone here this afternoon. I went over to the cabinet to light a cigarette with the lighter there." You glance at the huge cabinet. The lighter is on the top shelf.

"Suddenly I heard a sound behind me," Hamilton goes on. "An arm went around my neck, and a strong hand gripped my right arm. A hoarse voice asked me where the emeralds were. He threatened to choke me if I refused to tell him.

"All I could do was motion to the wall safe on the other side of the room. Then there was a blow on the side of my head. When I came to, he was gone—and so were my emeralds!"

"Can you describe the man?" you ask.

"No, he was behind me the whole time. He held me like a vise. That isn't much to go on, I'm afraid."

"No, it isn't," you say. "But I've heard enough to think you've staged a fake robbery for the insurance money!"

Why do you suspect Hamilton?

Hamilton claimed he did not see the thief, yet he said he was standing at the cabinet. If there had been a sound behind him, he could not have missed glancing into the huge mirror and seeing the man behind him.

The Case of the Bungled Break-Out

You are having dinner with old Martin Nolan, a retired warden of the state prison. He is regaling you with stories about some events that took place during his 30 years as warden.

"There was an attempted break that made the headlines," Nolan says. "That was 1956—it was February. The break was engineered by one of our lifers, Tom Hughes.

"He had been working for some time in our machine shop. He knew that on the first and 15th of every month, the prison gates were opened at exactly 8:35 A.M. for a switch engine to enter the siding that runs by the machine shop. Two guards stood at the open gates until the engine came out again with its load.

"Well, Hughes picked three other cons to break out with him. He made some knives out of scrap metal in the machine shop. On the 22nd of February, he gave them to his pals, and told them that a week from that day they were going to make their break.

"Each man was detailed to 'take care' of a guard. It was all timed to get them to the rail siding just as the engine pulled in.

"On the day planned, at exactly 8:30 A.M., the two machine-shop guards were knifed, and the break was on! The four men raced through the shop, out the door, down the steps, and around to the siding.

"Then came the shock—no engine! They panicked. It was no trouble for guards to take them back inside.

"It was a good plan," the ex-warden continues. "But Hughes made one mistake."

"I know," you say. "And I can tell you what it was."

What was Hughes' mistake?

Hughes forgot that the year of 1956 was a leap year, with 29 days in February. He planned the break for a week from February 22, thinking that would be March 1. But the day he picked was February 29.

The Case of the Burgled Bonds

The pale young man sitting next to your desk puffs nervously on a cigarette. You observe the neat plaid sport coat, narrow green bow tie, chocolate-brown trousers, and highly polished tan shoes.

"I'm Bradley Browne," the young man says, as he puts out his cigarette and lights another. "My uncle is Stephen Browne," he says. "His house has been burglarized. There was some negotiable bonds in the library safe. He's been out of town for 10 days, and I've been living in his home.

"He told me to keep an eye on things until he returned. Now it looks like I've failed him." Browne shakes his head sadly.

"The bonds were all stolen?" you ask.

"I'm sure. I was upstairs in the bathroom about a half hour ago. I was just about to shave when I heard a noise downstairs. I wiped the lather off my face and rushed downstairs, just in time to see a man run out of the library toward the front door. I yelled and ran after him.

"When I passed the library, the safe on the wall was open—so I suppose he got the bonds. By then he was climbing into a station wagon. I jumped into my car and tried to overtake him, but I lost him in the traffic."

"Did you get the license number?"

"No. I'm an awful fool, but I was too excited to think of that. I'm sorry. After I gave up the chase, I drove straight to your office."

"Don't you usually keep the downstairs doors locked?" you ask.

"Usually," he says. "I guess I must have forgotten."

"Can you describe the man?"

"Well, it happened so fast. He was about six feet tall. Tan suede jacket, dark-blue trousers, and a brown felt hat pulled over his face. That's all I can tell you. I'm going to hate telling all this to Uncle Steve."

"Instead of telling him this story," you say, "why don't you just put those bonds back into his safe!"

Why do you suspect Browne of staging the robbery?

According to Browne's story, he was shaving and had lather on his face when he heard the noise downstairs. He said he wiped off the lather, ran downstairs, chased the burglar, and drove straight to your office. If this were true, he would not have been wearing a coat and tie.

The Case of the Card-Party Killing

You and your good friend, Lieutenant Bill Marston, are in his office. The phone rings. It is a long conversation. He jots down notes on a pad as fast as he can. Then he hangs up and sits staring at his notes.

He turns to you with a smile. "That was Sergeant Dawson. He just covered a gang-killing over in the west end of town. Five hoodlums were having a little card party, and one of them shot and killed one of his playmates. Dawson gave me some notes on their activities. See if you can figure out who killed whom."

You study the notes:

"Daly played five games of handball with one of the innocent men this morning. The killer is Allison's cousin, and they grew up together. Ellington's hobby was photography. Casper is a fine handball player. He also used to be an expert pool player.

"The killer had an appendicitis operation two weeks ago. Billings only met Allison three weeks ago. Allison has been living with his mother for a year, and he's there now. Daly was quite a good piano player. Billings and Casper played pool together."

You look at Marston and say, "I know your two men."

Who are they?

Casper killed Ellington. Daly can't be the killer, since he played five games of handball this morning, and the killer was operated on two weeks ago. Allison is not the killer, but the killer's cousin. Billings is not the killer, for he met Allison for the first time three weeks ago. This leaves Casper and Ellington. Casper is obviously alive (he is a fine handball player), so he must have killed Ellington, the only other name mentioned.

The Case of the Collie Killing

The home of Mr. and Mrs. Joseph T. Collins has been burglarized, and their toothless old collie dog, King, brutally beaten to death.

"I don't mind the stolen jewelry so much," Mrs. Collins says. "But the senseless killing of poor old King! Everyone around here knows he wouldn't hurt a fly. He didn't even bark at strangers anymore. My friend Mrs. Miller was a witness. She was driving past our home when she saw a short, fat man run out of the yard."

You pin down two men that answer the description. One of them, Robert Stanton, lives across the street from the Collins. The other is a door-to-door salesman of cosmetics who was in the neighborhood.

"Surely you don't think I would rob my own friends!" Stanton exclaims. "I've known them for years!"

"No one is accusing you," you say.

"Don't you accuse me either," the salesman chimes in. "I'm just starting in this business. Today was my first visit to this town. If you think I'd be stupid enough to steal, you're crazy."

"We've always been friends," Stanton says. "I would feed their old dog, King, when he wandered over to my house."

After a few seconds, you point at one of the two men. You say, "You're coming with me to headquarters, on suspicion of burglary."

Which of the two men is it, and why?

The salesman. Since this was his first trip through the neighborhood, he did not know that the dog was perfectly harmless.

The Case of the Conked Clerk

You note the fresh white bandage on Tom Bell's head. Pale and exhausted, he slumps in the chair across from your desk.

Bell is a clerk in the local supermarket. He reports he was mugged and robbed while carrying the store's cash receipts to the bank.

"My boss, Mr. Henderson, gave me the job of carrying the money to the bank late this afternoon," he says. "Better than $1,500, I think.

"It's about five blocks from the store to the bank. Suddenly I heard a step behind me. Before I could turn around, I got a terrific smash on my head and blacked out.

"I got my senses back pretty quickly, though, because I caught sight of two men disappearing around the corner. Then I heard a car roaring off. All I had left was a big headache—the money was gone."

"I suppose there isn't any description you can give of the two robbers," you say.

"No, just that from behind they looked like pretty rough characters."

"Anything else?"

"Well," Bell says, "the license plate of their getaway car—it was this state, and it started with the letter *E*, then a *9* and an *8* and two more numbers I couldn't catch. Does that help?"

"Yes," you say. "It helps me a lot. How about telling me the true story now?"

Why do you suspect Bell's story?

Although Bell said he saw the robbers disappear around the corner and *heard* the sound of their car, he tried to give you the license number of the car. You suspect he is overeager to throw you a red herring, and that he staged the "robbery" himself.

13

The Case of the Curious Kidnapping

You have been informed that Allen Holden, kidnapped two weeks ago, will be returned to his home tonight. His father, a wealthy banker, paid $50,000 ransom to the kidnappers for his son's life. You are on your way to the Holdens' house for the happy reunion.

About half a block from the house, you see a figure walking briskly toward you along the dark street.

You look at your watch. It is 11:39. You come up behind the man just as he is about to enter the brightly lighted Holden home.

As you touch the man on his shoulder, he turns quickly toward you. You see he is a good-looking young man, very well dressed in a sharply pressed dark-gray suit, spotless white shirt, and carefully knotted blue tie.

"Allen?" you ask.

"Yes," he says nervously. "Come in—what do you want?"

You go inside, where the young man is greeted by his overwrought mother and father. Later, you all relax in the living room.

"I don't know at all where I was," Allen begins. "I was kept blindfolded the whole time, until they let me out of their car six or seven blocks from here.

"My hands were tied behind me, and I had to sleep in my clothes. They did shave me several times. They showed violence toward me only once. When I had almost rubbed my blindfold off against the edge of the bed I was lying on, someone hit me on the head."

You look at the swollen lump above Allen's left ear. "When was that?" you ask.

"About two days ago."

"Funny they didn't relieve you of that diamond ring you're wearing," you say.

"Well, I guess the ransom money was too much on their minds."

14

"I agree," you say. "The ransom money must have been on *someone's* mind. I think you can tell me a lot more about this than you have so far."

Why are you suspicious of Allen's story?

Allen told you he had lived and slept in his clothes for the entire two weeks, yet he was still dressed in a sharply pressed suit and spotless white shirt. If everything had happened as he told it, he would have presented a much more rumpled appearance.

The Case of the Dapper Dead-Beat

Doctor Dave Slade is an old and very good friend. Having nothing urgent to do today, you accompany him on his rounds through the town.

He stops before a neglected-looking house in a run-down area. "I'm going to make one last effort to collect a $100 fee from this man," he says. "Henry Sunderman has owed it to me for more than a year. He's been putting me off with one hard-luck story after another.

"But I happen to know that he always has plenty of money to play the horses. And yesterday he made quite a killing on a long-shot."

In answer to the doctor's knock, a dark-haired, dapper man answers. When he sees who it is, he says, "Sorry, Doc. I'm afraid things are still tough with me. I just can't seem to scrape $100 together."

Slade nods at you. You say, "We happen to know about your luck at the racetrack yesterday, Sunderman. I think you should give Dr. Slade his money before we have the law on you."

Sunderman gives you an evil look. Then, shrugging, he sits down to write out a check for $100. He hands it silently to Slade.

Back in the car, Slade says, "Well, I've got his check, all right, but it's worthless. I think I'll use it to get him into some trouble. You see, while he was writing it out, I saw his balance on the check stub. It was only $75. I guess I should have settled for the $75, but I didn't want to make any more fuss."

"If you're willing to settle for $75," you say, "you can have it by taking that check to the bank right now."

"How can I do that?" Slade asks. "The teller will return it to me, marked 'insufficient funds.'"

How can Slade cash the check and receive $75?

16

All he has to do is deposit \$25 of his own money in Henry Sunderman's account, bringing it up to \$100. Then he can cash his check.

The Case of Death by Drowning

You are in Charles Freeman's hospital room. He is lying in bed, a white bandage wrapped around his head. "Tell me what happened," you say. "How was your partner, Yates, killed?"

"A horrible tragedy," Freeman mutters. "Randy and I were on a weekend trip in my little cabin cruiser. Everything was fine, until we were preparing to anchor off the coast.

"Then it happened. Randy was throwing the anchor overboard. Somehow his foot got tangled in the line. The anchor's weight dragged him overboard. I rushed to the side of the boat. There he was, unconscious, hanging head-down just above the water. His head was no more than a foot above the water."

"Unconscious?" You raise an eyebrow.

"Yes. His head must have hit the side when he was carried over. Of course, I grabbed the line and pulled as hard as I could. I made a little progress—I had hold of Randy's feet. Suddenly, my feet slipped on the wet deck.

"I fell backward. My head hit the edge of the cabin door. I blacked out. I don't know how long I lay there.

"When I came to, my head was bleeding. I crawled to the side of the boat. Randy was still hanging there in the same position. But now his head was under water! The tide had come in!

"I shouted for help. Just as two men came running along the shore, I blacked out again. When I woke up here in the hospital, I found out that Randy had drowned."

"How was your business doing lately?" you ask. "Rumor has it that you and Yates weren't getting along."

"Well," Freeman says, "we did have a disagreement. We decided a week ago to dissolve our partnership. But there was no bitterness between us."

"Will you collect any insurance money?"

"Why, yes. We had $50,000 policies on each other. And now, if you don't mind, I could use some rest."

"You'll have plenty of time to rest," you say. "In jail!"

Freeman claimed the tide rose over Yates' head as he hung head-down over the side of the boat. This was impossible, since the boat would also have risen with the tide. As for Freeman's head wound, you suspect it was self-inflicted to make his story more convincing.

The Case of the Diamonds in the Dump

Patrolman Ron Cook trudges into your office, sits on a chair, mops the sweat off his brow with a huge handkerchief, and bursts out, "I'm really getting some beautiful assignments! I spent the last two hours in the town dump!"

"Want to talk about it?" you ask.

"Well," Cook says, "we got a call from this rich widow in the suburbs. Name of Mrs. Cordelia Henson. She has more jewels than she'll ever get around to wearing for the rest of her life.

"Anyway, she's got a particularly valuable diamond pendant, which for some crazy reason she kept in a red candy box. This afternoon she was baby sitting with her daughter's kids. After the kids went home, she straightened up some of the mess they had made.

"Well, when she threw out the papers, magazines, and other stuff, she also tossed the red candy box into the trash can. Before she knew what happened, the trash collectors had carted everything off to the dump. That's where I came in!"

"Any luck?" you ask.

"Only dirty hands and shoes. I ran into old Sam Appleby, though. He was scrounging around in the dump like always. I asked him if he'd run across a red candy box, and I thought my search had ended when he said he'd found it. But he said, 'Oh, yeah, I found it all right, but there weren't no diamonds in it.' Then he took it out of the little cart he always pushes—but no pendant."

"Well," you say, "if what you've told me is exactly what happened, you'd better pick up Sam Appleby and take him back to headquarters right away."

Why do you suspect Appleby?

According to what Cook told you, he made no mention of the candy box's contents when he questioned Appleby. Yet the old man volunteered the information that there were no diamonds in it.

The Case of the Dope-Ring Redheads

You and your friend, Lieutenant Jack Harrison, are in his office talking over what's been going on in his precinct. One problem is a local dope ring.

"Here is a report handed in by one of our rookie detectives after an intensive investigation," he says.

You take it and read: "The four members of the gang are Ethel Beard, Bert Holley, George Trainor, and Millie Jorgenson. One of them just got out of prison. Two of them are U.S. citizens, and two are foreigners.

"(1) Three days ago, the leader of the gang heard Millie Jorgenson and the ring's front having a fight over splitting profits.

"(2) The leader told Ethel Beard that he was in love with Millie's sister.

"(3) George Trainor, the front, and the member just out of prison were in a recent automobile accident.

"(4) We arrested Millie and her sweetheart in the gang's hide-out. We apprehended the other two when they were boarding a westbound plane.

"(5) One interesting fact is that the leader, the front, and Bert Holley are all redheads."

After you finish reading the report, you see Harrison grinning at you. "Well," he says, "can you tell me which of these four people is the leader of the dope ring, and who is the front?"

Who are they?

(1) Millie Jorgenson is neither the leader nor the front. (2) Ethel Beard is not the leader. (3) George Trainor is not the front. (4) Bert Holley is neither leader nor front. Therefore, George Trainor is the gang leader, and Ethel Beard is the front.

The Case of the Hotel-Room Heist

Diane Pettigrew, the very rich and very famous actress, has summoned you to her hotel room. She is hysterical about the robbery of her jewels. Much later, when she is somewhat calmer, she tells you her story.

"I was terrified," she says, "when this big tall man with a nylon-stocking mask over his face sneaked into my room this afternoon. He demanded the key to my jewel case, then ordered me into the bathroom. I was shaking uncontrollably, but I handed him the key.

"Then, before I went into the bathroom, another man came into the room. He was short and stocky, and also wore a stocking mask. They locked me in the bathroom. I could hear them moving around in the room and talking. Finally I heard them leave.

"About a half hour later, when my maid came in and let me out of the bathroom, my jewels were gone. Please, can you get them back for me?"

You make a thorough study of the hotel registrations. You question the employees. Your list of suspects is narrowed down to three men—Mark Addison, Richard Baylor, and Victor Cunningham.

You know that one of these three was the tall man who was first to enter the room. One of the three has been the tall man's partner in crime for several years. The third man has been a hotel employee for the past five years.

Other information you have picked up: Mark Addison registered in the hotel from Mexico City; Richard Baylor and the tall man, both college graduates, served time together in England for jewel theft; this has been the hotel employee's first criminal caper.

Given these facts, can you identify each of the suspects?

The hotel employee cannot be Mark Addison. Therefore he is either Baylor or Cunningham. Since Baylor served time in England with the tall man, we know the hotel employee must be Victor Cunningham. Since Cunningham has no criminal record and the tall man has, the tall man must be Mark Addison.

The Case of the Ice-Skating Incident

You are enjoying a winter vacation at a plush mountain resort. The temperature is a few degrees above zero, so you are happy to be next to a cozy fireplace.

Suddenly the front door bursts open. A wild-eyed, desperate-looking man stumbles in, shakes water from his clothes, and collapses on the floor. You recognize him—one of the guests, Roy Sanders.

Someone calls Dr. Cummings, the resort physician. He finally brings Sanders around.

Sanders gasps out his story. "My wife, Connie, and I are—were fond of ice-skating. After dinner tonight, we decided to go skating.

"We'd been out about an hour. My wife, who was skating 15 yards or so in front of me, suddenly cried out and fell through a big hole in the ice! Someone must have been cutting ice earlier.

"I managed to swerve in time to keep from falling in, too. I pulled off my skates and jumped in after her. I tried frantically to find her, but it was no use. By then I was so cold I could hardly pull myself out.

"I shouted for help as loud as I could, but there was no answer. So I started back to the lodge here."

Sanders seems to black out again. The doctor works on him.

You and two other men bundle yourselves up and hurry the half mile to the lake. You find the large hole in the ice that Sanders described. His skates are lying close by. You find no signs of his wife's body. You return to the lodge, carrying Sanders' skates.

When Sanders sees the skates, he collapses again. But before the doctor gets to him, you say, "You can stop the acting now, Sanders. I know your story was a lie. Tell me how you killed your wife."

Why do you suspect Sanders?

If everything had happened the way Sanders told it, he could not have walked a half mile through zero weather and then, on entering the lodge, have shaken water from his clothes. The water on his clothes would have been frozen.

The Case of the Lost Little Boy

As you drive along the street, a group of people in front of a modern apartment building attracts your attention. A woman in the center of the group is crying loudly.

You stop your car, get out, and ask one of the women what the problem is.

"Her little boy is missing," the woman says, "and she's afraid he's on one of the roofs!" The woman looks up at the top of the 15-floor building with horror. The roof adjoins the roofs of several other buildings.

"Why does she think he's up there?" you ask.

The frantic woman in the center turns to you. "Oh, I know he's up there!" she says. "He loves high places. He could run all over these flat roofs. My husband and I have often taken him up there. He loves to ride in the automatic elevator."

"How old is he?"

"Just three years old. He was playing on the sidewalk in front while I was inside talking to the manager. When I came out, he was gone!"

"Well," you say, "I think we should look for him on the apartment grounds."

"But the roofs!"

Some of the people help you to look. Sure enough, he is digging around in a flower bed behind the building. His mother takes him into her arms with a cry of joy.

Why were you so sure he had not gone up to the roof?

You knew that a three-year-old boy could not reach the "roof" or "15" button at the top of the elevator button-panel.

The Case of the Love-Lorn Lawyer

When you enter the law office of Henry Marsh, his dead body is facing you in the leather chair behind his desk. You walk around the desk to your right and see the bullet hole in the dead man's temple.

You turn to Carl Ferris, junior member of the law firm. He phoned you 15 minutes ago about the tragedy.

"I knew Henry was alone in his office tonight," the young man tells you. "I dropped in, thinking this would be a good time to discuss some personal matters with him. You can imagine how I felt when I found him like this!" He shudders.

You examine Marsh's desk and spot a typewritten letter. The initials "H.M." are scrawled in ballpoint ink at the bottom. The letter reads: "Life has become meaningless for me. I'm sorry. Good-bye."

You walk behind the corpse in the chair. On the other side, you see the right arm hanging beside the chair almost to the floor, still clutching the gun. You examine it. Yes, it has been recently fired.

"Did Marsh show any signs of depression lately?" you ask.

"No. He did seem preoccupied—after his fiancée, Loretta Pearson, decided not to marry him. That bothered him a lot. But I never suspected he was going to kill himself."

"As a matter of fact," you say, "he didn't. He was murdered. And I hope you can tell me more, Mr. Ferris."

Why do you think Marsh was murdered?

When you circled the victim's desk to your right, the bullet hole you saw was in the man's *left* temple. Then you saw the gun in his *right* hand.

The Case of the Madison-Street Mugging

You have volunteered your services to help stop the muggings in your town, so you are riding in a police cruiser with Officer Joe Sawyer. It is a brutally hot night. You are thankful for the car's air conditioning.

Suddenly, a call blares from the car's radio—a robbery on nearby Madison Street. Siren shrieking, you speed to the spot. You find a parked car with the engine and air-conditioning running.

Two men climb out of the car. They identify themselves as Jerry Padgett and Andy Harris. Padgett is a bill collector for a local loan agency. His friend Harris has come along as he makes some night collections.

"Just as we were pulling up in front of this apartment building," Padgett says, "two guys with stocking masks over their faces ran up on each side of the car. They jammed guns into our ribs and ordered us to hand over the money. I didn't hesitate a second—not with guns in our sides!

"I tossed my briefcase with the money in it out the window to the man on my side of the car. I sure hope you can do something about this. My boss isn't going to like it at all."

"I agree," you say. "Especially when I tell him that *you* staged this little caper!"

What makes you suspect Padgett of setting up the robbery?

Jerry Padgett told you the two robbers jabbed their guns into his and his friend's ribs. Since his car was air-conditioned, the windows must have been closed. It would have been impossible for the alleged robbers to press guns against their victims' bodies.

The Case of Miss Bishop's Bullet

Just before ringing the doorbell, you stop. The bullet hole in the door is directly in line with your chest. It reminds you of what happened to Frank Bishop. The same thing could happen to you. So you step to the side as you press the button.

"Who is it?" a female voice calls.

"The detective," you reply.

A tall, thin, gray-haired woman opens the door. She looks you over before letting you in. You follow her into the living room.

"I have good news for you," you say. "They removed the bullet. Your brother will probably pull through."

"That's just fine," she says, without emotion. "I suppose you want the whole story."

"Yes. All I know is that your brother is 52. He was going to be married next week, and now he has been accidentally shot—by you."

"That's so," Susan Bishop says. "Frank and I have lived here all our lives. Very happily, too—until he met that fast-living widow! He can't see that all she wants is his money."

"About the accident?" you say.

"Frank was out late again last night—out with *her*, I suppose. About midnight I heard someone at the front door. I called, 'Who's there?' several times. There was no answer.

"So I hurried back to my room and got my gun from the night table. We've had prowlers in this neighborhood, you know. I ran to the door again and called out once more. When there was no answer, I fired through the door—just to frighten whoever it was away.

"Imagine my horror when I heard a groan and the sound of a falling body. I opened the door and saw Frank lying there!" She buries her face in a lace handkerchief.

"Odd that he didn't answer when you called out," you remark.

"Well, he *may* have said something. I didn't hear him. My hearing isn't what it used to be. All I could see was the door knob turning, and I was so frightened!"

"I think you'd better pray for your brother's recovery," you say, "or it's a murder charge for you!"

Why do you think the shooting was not an accident?

Susan Bishop said that her being hard of hearing may have prevented her from hearing her brother reply to her calling, "Who's there?" But she had no trouble hearing your reply when you rang the bell. Also, she heard her brother's groan when she shot him and the sound of his falling body.

The Case of the Missing Money

"It's all gone! I don't know how much cash there was in the safe. I put $2,500 in it earlier this morning, and there was a bundle of money in there already."

Wealthy attorney Martin Crane mops his forehead. "I closed the safe and went out to buy a newspaper. I was gone only 15 minutes. When I returned, I don't know what made me look into the safe again, but I did. The money—all of it—had disappeared!

"Worst of all, the three people I always trusted implicitly are the only ones who know the combination. And they were all in the house this morning."

"Who are they?" you ask, taking notes.

"My niece, Anne Crane; my secretary, Priscilla Andrews; and Ted Johnson, my adopted son."

You question the suspects, jotting down the following notes:

Priscilla Andrews—about 40, very nervous and fidgety. Says she was in the kitchen making coffee. Knew nothing of the cash in the safe. Respects Mr. Crane too much to think of wronging him. Says she hasn't opened the safe for two weeks.

Anne Crane—pretty, blonde, a chain smoker. Well-known member of the jet set. Very cool and detached. Expresses regret over her uncle's loss, but says, "Five grand is a drop in the bucket to him." Was in her bedroom all morning, until summoned for questioning. Says the last time she opened the safe was a month ago when her uncle phoned from the office to ask about papers he left in the safe.

Ted Johnson—slick young man, a heavy gambler. No job for the last three months. Was in the garage all morning, making engine adjustments on his sportscar. Sorry about the stolen money, but shrugs it off as "the insurance company's worry." Can't remember the combination of the safe, but thinks he has it written down somewhere.

You study your notes. Then you tell Martin Crane, "Here's our suspect."

31

Anne Crane sounds like the guilty person. Crane himself did not know how much money was in the safe besides the $2,500, but Anne referred to a total of "five grand."

The Case of Miss Jarrington's Jewels

A frantic call from Miss Deborah Jarrington brings you to her home in the suburbs. The middle-aged woman meets you at the door of her tidy little cottage.

"I've been robbed!" she cries. "All my precious jewels—all of them—gone. And in broad daylight, too!"

She leads you to her bedroom in a back corner of the small, one-story cottage. The room is as neat as a pin. The only sign of an intruder is the open bottom drawer of the dresser. The contents are in disarray.

You open some of the other drawers. Finding nothing amiss, you turn to Miss Jarrington. "When and how did this happen?" you ask.

"After breakfast this morning, I went out to the side yard to do some weeding in my garden. It's on the other side of the house from my bedroom. I thought I might have heard some strange sounds from inside the house, but I didn't think too much about it. When I finally came into the house and into the bedroom—the drawer was open—all my jewels were gone!

"The thief must have climbed in and out through the window there. The only entrance, besides the side door where I was working, is the front door. I would have seen anyone entering or leaving."

You lean out the window of the bedroom. Sure enough, below the window in the flower bed there are footprints. Even now, they are half full of water. The soil around the prints has been well cultivated.

"Were the jewels valuable?" you ask.

"To me they were much more valuable than the $40,000 they were insured for," Miss Jarrington replies. "They've been in my family for generations."

"Who knew you kept these jewels here?"

"No one. Only the insurance man knew. No one else knew I had anything so precious in my house. I've never even had a maid. I didn't want a strange woman in my house who might find my jewels."

You think for a few minutes. Then you say, "I don't think the insurance company will pay this claim. What did you do with the jewels, Miss Jarrington?"

Why do you think Miss Jarrington has staged a fake robbery?

According to Miss Jarrington, no one knew about her jewels or where she kept them. Yet only the bottom drawer of her dresser was searched by the "intruder." Also, despite the muddy foot-prints under the window, the room was still immaculate. There should have been some mud in the room if a thief came in by the window.

The Case of the Murdered Magistrate

You drop in late at night for your usual cup of coffee with your friend, Bruce Bennett. The rich old judge lives on the edge of town with his nephew, 23-year-old Charles Pope.

Tonight, however, things are not going to be usual. No one answers your ring. And in the study you are greeted by a horrible sight.

Bruce Bennett is lying on the floor in the middle of the room. One look tells you he is dead. The protruding tongue, contorted face, and bruises on his scrawny neck testify to the fact that he was strangled.

You kneel over the body to feel for any possible heartbeat. None. From the still warm temperature of the body, you decide it must have happened very recently. You look around the room and note the overturned chair, the papers scattered on top of Bennett's desk, and the curtains blowing from the open window behind the desk.

You walk across the hall to the nephew's room. After knocking and getting no response, you open the door. It is pitch dark. Unable to find a wall switch, you pick out the outline of a table lamp against the window.

You make your way carefully across the room, fumble for the lamp switch, jerk your hand away, finally find the switch and flip it on.

You see Charles Pope sprawled out on his bed, mouth open, eyes closed, breathing heavily. You grab his arm, and he sits up.

"What—who? Oh, it's you," he says. "What's the idea of barging into my room and waking me up?"

"Your uncle is dead," you say.

"Oh no! Uncle Bruce dead! And here I was sleeping when I could have helped him! How did it happen?"

"I think you can answer that question for *me*," you say.

Why do you suspect Charles Pope?

You know that Charles Pope was only pretending to be asleep. As you fumbled for the lamp switch, you jerked your hand away—because the bulb was still hot.

The Case of the Nasty Neighbor

Your phone rings at nine in the morning. An excited male voice launches into a tirade. "I just got an anonymous threatening letter in the mail, postmarked yesterday. Even though the coward didn't put his name on it, I know who he is—one of my neighbors.

"I had some trouble with his dog. When he didn't do anything about it, I reported him to the police. Since then he's been bad-mouthing me. And now this letter—telling me he's going to get even with me!"

You manage to calm him down with the promise of an investigation. An hour later, Sergeant Joe Keller stalks into the office.

"I'm late this morning," he says. "I had to stick around at home waiting for the mail. I was expecting a check. But the mail was almost an hour late. It didn't come until about 9:45."

You tell him, "I had a call from a guy who lives on your street— Sam Taylor. He claims he got an anonymous letter this morning. He's accusing another one of your neighbors, Albert Berger, of having mailed it."

"I know them both," Keller says. "Taylor is a troublemaker who will argue with anybody. Albert Berger is one of the nicest people I know. He wouldn't do something like that—even to Sam Taylor."

"Well, Taylor was lying, anyway," you say.

How do you know Taylor lied?

It was nine o'clock when Taylor phoned you about getting the threatening letter in the mail. But Sergeant Keller, who lives on the same street, told you the mail that morning did not arrive until about 9:45.

37

The Case of the Pantomime Pilferer

"Only two people in the world—my nephew and my secretary—knew I kept large amounts of money in my safe at home. And only these two young men knew the safe's location, behind a wood panel in my study. It's always been one of my most closely-kept secrets."

Wealthy attorney Daniel Harding has summoned you to report a robbery of $15,000 in cash. "Much as I hate to say this, one of these two has to be guilty—but which one?" He shakes his head sadly.

"Shortly after I put the money into the safe early this afternoon, a masked man in a shabby gray suit, with a hat pulled over his face, stalked into the room. He wore a pair of white work gloves and carried a gun. He didn't say a word—just motioned me over to the safe. He pointed at the spot where the secret button is and, without a single word, forced me to get the money out and hand it over to him!

"Then, still without speaking, he made me understand that I was not to move until after he left. A few seconds after he ran out of the room, I phoned you."

You interview the young men separately. As Harding's nephew, Richard Parks, enters, you notice his flaming red hair, freckled face and hands, and the strength and grace of his movements.

He tells you, "I was upstairs asleep in the guest room until I heard Uncle Dan's shouts down here in the study. I admit I owe a bit of money here and there—but I am certainly not a thief!"

Next is the dark, handsome secretary, Joseph Arlen. He is about the same height and build as Richard Parks.

"I was busy all afternoon visiting clients," he says. "Of course, I knew about the money Mr. Harding usually kept in the house. He's always treated me fair and square, though. I would never do a thing like this to him. I was in trouble when I was a teenager,

38

but not since then! Mr. Harding knows all about it, though. It didn't make any difference to him. He trusted me."

After Arlen leaves the room, you turn to Harding and say, "One of these men has to be the robber, and I'll tell you which one!"

Who is he?

Richard Parks. There was no need for the robber to wear gloves. He touched nothing except the money. Also, since he lived or worked in the house, his fingerprints would naturally be all over the house. You suspect Richard Parks of wearing gloves for the purpose of concealing his tell-tale freckles!

The Case of the Pharmacist's Fatality

A high wind has been raging through the city all night. It whips your coat around your legs, and you keep a tight grip on your hat. You have just passed a drugstore when suddenly two shots ring out! You wheel around and decide they came from inside the drugstore.

You race through the front door of the store. Sprawled on the floor next to the prescription counter is the white-coated, bulky body of a middle-aged man. Kneeling beside him is a frightened-looking young man in gray slacks and a dark jacket. His long, silky-looking hair is neatly combed in ducktail fashion. "He ran out the back door," the young man blurts out.

You run out the back door and scan the alley. It is deserted. You go back inside.

With your handkerchief, you pick up the gun that is lying next to the body. You sniff. It has been fired very recently. You call headquarters and leave orders for the police to block off the area.

Then you turn to the young man for his story. "My name is Don Stratton. I live in an apartment in the next block. I had just come in here tonight for some cigarettes. Right away, I saw something was wrong. There was a man standing in front of Mr. Hudson, the pharmacist who works here. When he heard me come in, he spun around and I saw he had a gun.

"Then Mr. Hudson made a grab for the gun. It went off—two shots—and Mr. Hudson fell. I guess the robber panicked, because he threw the gun down and ran out the back door—just before you came in."

"Did you get a good look at him?" you ask.

"No, everything happened too fast. All I can say is that he was wearing a gray overcoat, and had a gray hat pulled down low over his face. He was kind of tall—about six feet."

"That's a good description of someone who doesn't exist," you say. "I think I'm looking at the killer right now!"

Despite the very high winds outside, you have noticed how neatly combed Stratton's hair is. This means he must have been inside the store with Hudson longer than he has told you. If he had just come in, as he said, his hair would have been in a wind-blown, messy state.

The Case of the Purloined Loan Money

"Give me a description of the robber," you say to Harry Robinson, manager of the Tender Heart Loan Company.

"Well, he was tall, good-looking, with long, dark-brown hair. His topcoat was buttoned up, with the collar up around his neck. He had dark-brown trousers, black shoes, and his belt buckle had the initial *W* on it."

"How did the robbery happen?" you ask.

"I was counting the day's receipts in the office tonight. Suddenly, there he was, gun in hand. He ordered me to put my hands up.

"He stuffed the money into a shopping bag. Then he shoved me into my chair, tied me up, gagged me, and left. It took me a while to get loose. Then I called you."

"Did you notice anything else about the man?"

"Only that he was not in a hurry. He seemed quite at ease. Oh yes, he was very polite, too."

"I think this has gone far enough, Robinson," you say. "It appears to me that this robbery was staged by you!"

What has led you to this conclusion?

Robinson told you the robber's topcoat was buttoned up. Therefore, he could not have seen a *W* on the robber's belt buckle.

The Case of the Rifled Ring

The hotel manager meets you in the lobby of the hotel. He is worried about unfavorable publicity because of the robbery in his hotel. "I wasn't on duty at three o'clock in the morning when the diamond was taken," he says. "This is the first incident of this kind in *my* hotel!"

He takes you up to Mrs. Hayes' suite. She is a beautiful young widow. As she speaks, she dabs at her eyes with a handkerchief.

"The robbery was right here in this room!" she says. "I'm glad just to be alive. The diamond ring was very dear to me—not because it cost my husband so much money, but because it was his last gift to me."

"I understand," you say. "Can you tell me how it happened?"

"Well, I retired at midnight. At three in the morning, I heard a noise in this room. My bedroom is off the hallway, so I got up quietly and tiptoed through the pitch dark to the sitting room here.

"I intended to switch the light on suddenly and surprise the intruder. Without warning, a hand grabbed my wrist and another hand closed over my mouth. A voice whispered, 'Don't make a sound!' I couldn't see his face or anything else. The drapes were all closed, and no light came in from outside.

"He pulled me over to my vanity table, picked up my precious ring, warned me again to keep quiet, and ran out! My nerves finally gave way, and I fainted. It wasn't until early this morning that I phoned the manager.

"The ring is insured, of course, but that won't make up for . . ."

"Just a minute," you say. "I think you can forget about the insurance. If you need money so badly, why didn't you take the ring to a pawn shop?!"

Why do you think Mrs. Hayes staged a fake robbery?

43

You don't think she would have attempted to surprise an intruder by suddenly switching on a light. She would have been more likely to scream or to phone for help. And, in the darkness she described, she couldn't have stated the exact time of the robbery, and the "robber" wouldn't have been able to spot the ring on the vanity table.

The Case of the Rubbed-Out Racketeer

Your car crawls at a snail's pace this evening through one of the worst fogs in the city's history. Most of the time you have to stick your head out the window to see the white center line of the street. You finally arrive at the large suburban home of racketeer Pete Moss.

When he answers your ring at his door, Moss's face indicates his displeasure at seeing you. He reluctantly lets you in.

"As you know," you begin, "we've been working for some time to stop the operation of a counterfeiting ring in this area—an operation that we're sure you have a big hand in.

"So far we haven't had enough evidence to indict you—until yesterday. We got a phone call from one of your lieutenants, Vincent Hatton. He said he was fed up with the whole deal and was going to blow the whistle on you. He was coming down to our office today to tell everything he knew."

You pause, watching Moss's face. "The big trouble is," you say, "that Vincent didn't show up. He was killed late this afternoon— shot through the head in his apartment."

Moss looks at you. "Yeah, I learned about it a few minutes ago while I was on my way home from working out at the gym. I saw the headline when I drove past a newspaper stand a block from here."

"So now you know why I'm here," you say.

"Sure. You think I made the hit. But Vince had nothing on me—and neither do you!"

"Well, if you're not involved in Hatton's murder," you say, "I'm sure you won't mind telling me the truth about how you found out he was dead."

Why do you think Moss is lying?

Because of your own experience a few minutes ago in the dense fog, you know that Moss could not have seen the headline in the newspaper stand.

45

The Case of the Scared Stockbroker

You arrive at Amos Caruthers' beautiful suburban home. The middle-aged stockbroker meets you at the door. He nervously mops perspiration from his forehead with a wadded handkerchief.

"All that cash—more than $25,000—stolen from under my nose!" he exclaims. "I haven't touched anything in the study. I left everything just as I found it. Wait till you see the mess."

He throws open the door of a room that leads off the front hall. At first all you see is what appears to be an orderly-looking study. There is a desk with neatly arranged piles of papers, and some neat bookshelves.

Walking further into the room, you see what Caruthers meant by "mess"—a large, open safe with papers, documents, and torn boxes scattered inside and on the floor in front of it.

"I was working in here this evening," Caruthers explains. "I went into the kitchen for a snack. While I was eating, I thought I heard some suspicious noises.

"I went quietly through the hall. The door to this room was partly open. Although I saw immediately what had happened, I couldn't see or hear anyone inside. I was pretty sure the thief was gone, but I still didn't dare enter the room.

"So I hurried to the living room and called you. Then I called my insurance company."

"You're covered for this loss?" you ask.

"Oh, yes. I don't stand to lose anything. But I still hope you—"

"I don't think the insurance company stands to lose anything either," you say. "There's something about your story that just doesn't work."

Why don't you believe Caruthers' story?

Caruthers told you that without entering the room, he saw immediately through the partly opened doorway what had happened to his safe. But he could not have done this—you yourself could see nothing unusual until you had walked into the room itself.

The Case of the Seaside Suicide

Police Chief Sam Lawton waves his hand over the objects on his desk. "I can't help feeling this is a hoax. But we have to act on it anyway—we can't be sure."

You run your hand through the clothes on the desk. "This is what you found on the beach?" you ask. "These clothes and the note?"

Lawton nods and hands you the typewritten note.

You read: "I have been meditating here on the beach for more than an hour. I have decided to write this letter to whomever it might interest—the final words of a passing soul. My cares and troubles have continued to heap up until now, when I feel the best solution is just to leave them all behind me. Farewell, everyone!"

Chief Lawton says, "A patrolman brought the note and clothes in early this morning. He was on the boardwalk near the beach and noticed a set of footprints going across the beach. Then he saw the prints of bare feet going into the water, the pile of clothes, and this note. No other footprints were on the beach. It's a lonely area during the cold season. In a minute, I'll call the Coast Guard to search the water in the bay."

"Don't bother," you say. "This suicide note is a fake."

Why do you think that?

According to the letter, the writer decided to write his note on the beach after an hour of meditation. But the note was type-written, and there was no typewriter on the beach. You decide that the hoaxter typed the letter at home, left it on the beach, made his set of footprints leading into the water, and then waded further along the beach before going back to dry land.

The Case of the Shunned Ship

You are at a restaurant with your friend, Captain Robert Rushton. His weather-worn face is marked with worry about the Board of Inquiry investigating a recent occurrence at sea.

"Imagine," he says, "*me* being accused of leaving another ship in distress! Doesn't my record mean anything?"

"Why don't you tell me about it?" you say.

"We were steaming south," he says. "The sea was as flat as a table—not a breath of air stirring. Shortly after noon, our lookout reported a vessel ahead. He made it out to be the *S. S. Miranda*.

"It seemed to be laying to, or at least moving along very slowly. We passed within a mile or so of it, but there seemed to be nothing unusual—no sign of distress. So we kept on our course. I heard nothing further about it, until last week when I made port."

"What's the case against you?"

"Captain Moeller, of the *Miranda*, claims he was in distress at the time. He says they lost all power aboard ship, so their radio was useless. And they had used up all their distress rockets.

"When my ship came along, he ordered a flag hoisted upside down—you know, the international signal of distress. He says he was 'horrified' to see us move on and away. Moeller would like to see me stripped of my master's papers." Your friend shakes his head mournfully.

"I don't think there's any danger of your losing your papers," you say. "Just remind the Board of one thing."

What "one thing" will win the case for Captain Rushton?

The day was calm, with "not a breath of air stirring," so the distress flag would have hung limply. Your friend, passing a mile or so away, could not have seen whether the flag was hanging upside down or not.

49

The Case of the Slashed Satchel

Arthur Cameron is slumped in a chair at the Leave-You-A-Loan Company when you arrive. A doctor has just finished bandaging a huge cut on his forehead. On the floor is a leather bag with its side slit wide open.

"This was the most brazen robbery I ever heard of," says the company's manager, Martin Phelps. "The first robbery we've had, and in broad daylight, too."

You ask Cameron to tell his story. "Well," he begins, "I make regular trips to the bank to deposit our cash. I've been doing it for two years. I carry it in this leather bag." He points to the slashed bag on the floor.

"This afternoon," he goes on, "I was on my usual route—first over Main Street, then north on Chestnut, which is a side street. Suddenly, as I was passing an alley, I was hit on the head from behind.

"I must have passed out for a while. When I came to, I was lying in the alley. The bag was next to me—empty! I came right back to the office, and Mr. Phelps phoned you."

"You didn't get a look at the assailant?" you ask.

"No. I didn't see him and I didn't hear anything. Evidently no one saw the robbery either, because I was all alone when I came to."

"Of course, we're insured for the loss of the $5,000," puts in the manager, "but I hope you'll catch the thief."

You examine the leather bag. "It must have been a very sharp knife," you say. Then you inspect the lock on the top catch of the bag. It is still intact.

"It was a good try," you say to Cameron. "Now suppose you tell us what you did with the money!"

Why do you suspect Cameron?

First, Cameron claimed he was struck from behind. Yet the wound was on his forehead. He must have inflicted it on himself. Second, robbers would not be likely to take the time in daylight to cut open the bag at the scene of the robbery. They would have escaped *with* the bag.

The Case of the Sporting-Goods Stickup

Early this morning, you are walking down Main Street. It is deserted except for your friend, Sam Graham. He is unlocking his sporting-goods store, and invites you in for coffee.

Following him into his office at the back of the store, you find a surprise. His sales clerk, Kevin Connell, is all tied up on a chair, a handkerchief knotted over his mouth.

You look over the room. The door of the large safe is open, the floor littered with papers. Even the chair on which young Connell is squirming rests on some papers from the safe.

You and Graham untie Connell. He tells you the story. "I got here a little early this morning. I had just opened the safe when I heard, 'Put your hands up and don't talk.'"

"Did you see him?" you ask.

"Yeah—a short guy with a stocking mask over his face. He had a gun. He pushed me into the chair and tied and gagged me. Then he went through the safe, tossing out papers until he found the money."

"How long was he gone before we got here?" asks Sam Graham.

"Not more than five minutes. I was still in a state of shock when you came in. He had warned me not to move, and he sounded like he meant business! Of course, I couldn't have moved if I'd tried. I was really trussed up."

"Well," you say, "I don't think you'll have any trouble moving now. You're coming with me to headquarters. You told a good story—but not good enough."

Why do you think Connell is lying?

According to Connell, the thief did not begin looting the safe until after he had tied him to the chair. Yet you found the chair on which he was tied so securely resting *on top of* some of the papers from the safe. And Connell said he was too well tied to move.

The Case of the Startled Socialite

A maid shows you into the brightly lighted living room. Margaret Van Leer, the well-known socialite, has been waiting for you.

"My jewels!" she cries hysterically. "All my lovely jewels—gone—stolen! Even though they are insured, the money won't begin to compensate me for their sentimental value. They were given to me by my dear, departed husband."

"Suppose you try to tell me what happened," you say.

"I was sitting alone here in the living room, watching television. Suddenly, I heard the sound of running feet on the footpath through my garden at the side of the house. It was about 9:30 P.M., I think.

"I turned my head from my chair in the middle of the room. Through the picture window I saw him! He was tall, and wore a dark-blue jacket and a soft plaid hat with a little feather stuck in the band.

"He was running along the path through the garden. He was at least 50 feet away by then. I screamed, and Janet—my maid—ran in.

"Our first thought was—my jewels! We hurried up to my bedroom and saw immediately that he had been there. My things were thrown all over the place. My jewel case was on top of my dressing table—empty!"

Your eyes survey the room. You ask, "Do you always keep this room as brightly lighted as it is now?"

"Oh yes. I don't like dimly lighted rooms. Besides, it's much easier on my eyes while I'm watching television."

"Well," you say, "I don't think the insurance company will be very easy on you."

Why are you suspicious of Mrs. Van Leer's story?

A person sitting in the middle of a brightly lighted room at night, looking out through a window into the darkness, cannot see a great distance—especially to discern the color of a man's clothing or the fact that he is wearing a "plaid hat with a little feather stuck in the band." It is also doubtful that a person listening to television could hear the sound of running feet 50 feet away from the house.

The Case of the Stolen Stamps

You arrive at the scene of the terrible fire. Most of old Joshua Adams' mansion is destroyed. Adams himself is dead from smoke inhalation.

Adams' nephew, Tom Trenton, tells you he arrived from out of town two hours ago, after the fire was under control. He seems grief-stricken over his uncle's death.

You follow Trenton into the ruins of the old house. Down in the cellar you find an old iron safe standing upright in the rubble.

"How about that!" Trenton exclaims. "That safe was in Uncle Josh's bedroom on the second floor! It dropped through two floors!"

He opens the safe. You see small, tidy stacks of loose stamps. These must be Adams' famous collection.

Since you are a collector yourself, you look through the stamps. You are shocked that the stamps in the safe seem to be worth only about $7,000. Adams' collection had been valued at no less than $200,000! You know that he kept all his stamps in stacks, not albums.

"Was the safe opened before you got here?" you ask Trenton.

"Oh no. The first time it was touched was when I opened it for you a few minutes ago."

"I think I'll take you to headquarters," you say, "under suspicion of robbery—and possibly of arson and murder too!"

What aroused your suspicions of Trenton?

You are suspicious because of the "small, tidy stacks of loose stamps" on the floor of the safe. Since the safe fell through two floors of the house, the stamps should have been scattered all over the safe. You think Trenton took out the most valuable stamps. Then, thoughtlessly, he arranged the stamps in stacks as was his uncle's custom.

55

The Case of the Summerhouse Slaying

On the lawn outside the screened-in rear porch of the sum-merhome, you examine the bullet hole through the copper screening. Brushing your hand across the screen, you cry out in pain. Your forefinger is bleeding from the sharp wires protruding around the bullet hole.

You wrap your handkerchief around the finger. Entering the porch, you look down at the body of Daniel Stevenson, president of Stevenson and Blair, a brokerage firm.

Stevenson is slumped in a chair. Apparently a bullet fired from a gun outside the porch pierced the man's heart as he sat facing the lawn outside.

"Dan dropped in to discuss business," explains Keith Blair, the owner of the summerhome. "We were sitting here on the porch with some drinks. Things haven't been going well at the office, and Dan was worried.

"I glanced out toward the yard and I saw a man partly hidden by a tree. He was pointing a gun this way. Before I could warn Dan, the man fired. Dan fell forward—dead!

"I ran out onto the lawn, but the man had disappeared. I can't describe him—it happened so quickly."

"Do you suspect anyone—someone who hated your partner enough to kill him?"

"No," says Blair. "Of course, Dan was a hard man to get along with. But as to telling you who could hate him enough to kill him. . . ." Blair shakes his head.

"On the contrary," you say. "I'm sure you *can* tell me—much more than you have so far!"

Why do you suspect Keith Blair's story?

Blair told you the shot was fired from outside the porch, yet your finger was nicked by the wires in the screen around the bul-let hole protruding *outward*—proving that the bullet went through the screen from inside the porch.

The Case of the Supercilious Secretary

A smug-looking young woman, Sarah Stewart, stalks into your office. She thrusts a piece of paper at you. "Just look at this piece of garbage," she snorts.

You read it: "Miss Stewart, your loose tongue is going to get you into big trouble. Prepare for the worst—very soon!" Typewritten . . . and no signature. Naturally.

"A person has to be nuts to write poison like that," Miss Stewart says. "I think I know just who would be batty enough to do it—my boss, Sybil Greenstreet!"

"What leads you to that conclusion?" you ask.

"She's the only one I know with a grudge against me. I happen to know a lot more about the firm than *she* does. I've managed to show her up several times in the office. I knew she was miffed. But I didn't think she would stoop as low as this."

A half hour later you are in Sybil Greenstreet's office. "I'm here in regard to a letter that one of your employees, Sarah Stewart, received today," you say.

"That arrogant young know-it-all!" The middle-aged woman is quivering with anger. "She thinks she could run the company by herself! It's about time someone threatened her. Maybe this will frighten the conceit out of her."

"Maybe so," you say. "But I can't agree with your methods."

Why do you suspect her of sending the letter?

Ms. Greenstreet convicted herself with her own words. Before you mentioned the kind of letter Sarah Stewart had received, Ms. Greenstreet broke in with a tirade in which she revealed that she knew the letter was a threat.

The Case of the Teenage Terror

Tom Harrison's drugstore has been robbed. More than $300 in cash was taken, and Harrison was left bleeding and unconscious on the floor.

You suspect a gang of five teenage boys who are frequent patrons of the store. They were all in the vicinity on the night of the holdup.

A witness on the opposite side of the street swears he saw one of the boys run out of the store. But it was dark, and since all the boys wear the same blue T-shirts, he can't identify which boy he saw.

You have questioned the druggist briefly in his hospital room. He cannot tell who his attacker was because he was struck without warning from behind.

You have collected facts about the five teenagers—Johnny Abbott, Dick Bantley, Chuck Collins, Eddie Dale, and Pete Eversole: (1) Abbott and Collins both claim they were swimming at the town pool the night of the holdup. (2) The robber and Dale both graduated from the same high school in June. (3) Dale and Abbott were stars of their opposing high-school basketball teams last season. (4) Eversole and Bantley teamed up in a three-legged race at a picnic last weekend. During the race they tripped, and Eversole suffered two fractured bones in his ankle. (5) Bantley and Dale were suspected of a service station holdup three months ago and questioned thoroughly. They were released for lack of evidence. (6) The robber has been going steady with Bantley's sister for five months.

Who beat and robbed Tom Harrison?

(1) Eddie Dale is eliminated as the robber. (2) Abbott cannot be the robber. (3) Pete Eversole cannot have run out of the drugstore. (4) Dick Bantley cannot be the robber. (5) This leaves Chuck Collins as your prime suspect.

The Case of the Weeping Widow

Wealthy retired businessman John Benham, aged 70, lies dead, a bullet hole in his forehead. The body is near a window on the first floor of his mansion. Nothing else in the room looks unusual. In the next room, his hysterical wife is being comforted by neighbors, while detectives search the area.

After she calms down, you ask her what happened. Wiping a tear from her cheek, she says, "It was after dinner. I cooked it, because today was a holiday and I gave the servants the day off.

"John and I were standing at the front window, which was up, enjoying the evening breeze. Suddenly I heard a sharp sound and saw a flash from the top floor of the house across the street. John collapsed—he'd been shot!"

"How tall was your husband?" you ask.

"Five feet ten."

The house across the street is vacant, with a "For Rent" sign. You push open the back door and climb up to the top floor. You look from each window across and down to the window where Benham had been standing.

You return to the Benham house. "And now, Mrs. Benham," you say, "I want you to tell me the truth."

Why are you suspicious of Mrs. Benham's story?

Because of Benham's height, he could not have been shot through the forehead without one of the panes of the window being broken.

59